For my parents   *H.P.*

The return of the sparrow   *K.H.*

For my mother   *I.G.*

Text copyright © 2006 by Hans Post and Kees Heij

Illustrations copyright © 2006 by Irene Goede

Originally published in the Netherlands by Lemniscaat b.v. Rotterdam, 2006,

under the title *Mus*

All rights reserved

Printed in Belgium

First U.S. edition, 2008

CIP data is available

Lemniscaat

An Imprint of Boyds Mills Press, Inc.

815 Church Street

Honesdale, Pennsylvania 18431

Hans Post & Kees Heij / Irene Goede

Sparrows

Lemniscaat
Honesdale, Pennsylvania

It is spring. Two
House Sparrows
made a nest under
broken roof tiles. The
nest holds five eggs.

A crack in the egg

Push, sparrow! The egg breaks. …

Here is a sparrow chick.
That was hard work, even with a beak!

The nest has become full.

The baby sparrows are very hungry. To feed her babies, the mother collects small insects that live on plants.

The mother knows which insects to give her young.

Bread is not good for young birds.

Fully grown sparrows like to eat seeds, and there are plenty in the summer.

A Crane Fly is very nice to eat, so the father catches it for his young.

Wheat

Barley

Oats

The male sparrow collects
more food for the chicks. There!
On the front of a car!
Lots of dead flies and insects.

The mother feeds her chicks. They always have their beaks wide open, waiting for food.

The mother sparrow removes the broken eggshells from the nest.

The father sparrow helps to clean as well by throwing the poop out of the nest.

One sparrow fledgling flaps her wings faster and faster until she flies. She is scared, danger is everywhere. …

Next door, a black cat hungrily gazes at the sparrows.

In a garden chair, a big tomcat lies asleep, ignoring the birds.

Crows and magpies
also have young, which
attack the sparrows.

Cars drive past the garden.
Watch out, sparrow!

When they are old enough,
the fledgling sparrows sleep
outside of the nest, and they
hide in the bushes.
They are happy in there.

The night also brings danger.
Owls are out hunting.

Rats and weasels are also
on the prowl.

Autumn has arrived!
The sparrows must leave
the garden to find food.

In the street lies dog poop.
One sparrow finds food in it!

Another sparrow lights on some
fresh horse manure. ...

So much food can be found near the
barns and silos. The sparrows don't
need to look hard.

It is winter and the snow covers
the ground. The sparrows find food
at a bird feeder.

Crow

Greenfinch

Fieldfair

Wood Pigeon

Blackbird

Dunnock

Starling

Magpie

This sparrow tries to eat from the peanut string but finds it hard, unlike the chickadee.

This sparrow must hold on tight to feed on a net filled with food. The blue titmouse is very good at this.

When the sparrow has eaten enough, she fluffs out her feathers to keep warm.

The snow has gone and the warm spring has arrived. This sparrow plucks petals and the stigma from a yellow crocus. Will she eat them?

This sparrow sees a male
that she likes.
He makes a
beautiful nest
in a tree.

What is the male sparrow doing?

He is attracting a female sparrow in a
courtship display that lasts a long time.

The new nest is almost
ready—a bit of moss here,
a tuft of wool there. …

The male sparrow builds the nest
out of straw, grass, and brushwood.
He lines it with moss.

The pigeon has a loose
feather in his wing. The
sparrow takes it to use in
his nest.

Sparrows build nests in strange places.

In a statue, nice and dry.

On a lighted wall sign,
nice and warm.

In an old swallows' ncst,
nice and easy.

Hey! That's mine!

Keep away from that, sparrow,
or you'll set fire to your nest!

One male pairs with a female
on a clothesline.

Another male finds a sandpit in the garden.
He takes a nice dust bath.

The female sparrow
lays her eggs in the nest.

She bathes in the pond,
which is cool and not too deep,
then dries her feathers in the sun's warmth.

The sparrow chicks have hatched.
Perhaps one will come to live in
your garden. Who knows?

House Sparrows in North America

This book shows House Sparrows living in Europe. That's where the birds came from before any of them lived in North America.

Some people brought House Sparrows here in 1850. Since then, the birds have spread across the land, probably because they can live on farms or in cities.

In 1870, people also brought Eurasian Tree Sparrows to America. But these birds live around farmlands and are found only in a small area near St. Louis, Missouri.

In North America, many people say House Sparrows are pests. These people love bluebirds. Both House Sparrows and bluebirds build their nests in small spaces, such as a hole in a tree. House Sparrows chase bluebirds away from these nesting places and use them for their own nests.

But the great American naturalist Roger Tory Peterson loved House Sparrows. He saw that they were here to stay. Now many people try to make room for both bluebirds and House Sparrows.

Eurasian Tree Sparrow   Male House Sparrow

Do you know about the sparrow?

It does not run. It hops.

It can live for seven years.

It has a good sense of smell and can see colors.

It can weigh as much as seven sugar cubes.

It has more than 3,500 feathers.

The heart of a sparrow beats eight hundred times in a minute. The heart of a person beats only seventy times in a minute.